Irish
Medieval Figure Sculpture
1200–1600

Irish Medieval Figure Sculpture

1200–1600

A study of Irish tombs
with notes on costume and armour

JOHN HUNT

with assistance and
contributions from
Peter Harbison

with photographs
by David H. Davison

Volume 2
(Plates)

IRISH UNIVERSITY PRESS   SOTHEBY PARKE BERNET

ISBN 0 85667 012 X

Published jointly by
Irish University Press Ltd., 81 Merrion Square, Dublin 2
Sotheby Parke Bernet Publications Ltd., 34 & 35 New Bond Street, London W1

PRINTED IN HOLLAND
AND BOUND IN THE REPUBLIC OF IRELAND

for Putzel

Contents

Note

The three hundred and forty plates in this volume illustrate the text and catalogue contained in Volume I. Each illustration has a descriptive caption and a catalogue number for cross-reference. The plates are arranged by subject (knights, civilian males, tomb surrounds, etc.) within the three phases covered.

Period I (1200–1350) corresponds roughly to the latter part of the Norman invasion and the subsequent peak of Anglo-Norman penetration;
Hiatus (1350–1450) is the phase, after the Black Death, of native Irish revival;
Period II (1450–1570) is the final phase which developed after the earldoms of the Middle Nation had sufficiently established themselves and society reached its zenith in the comparatively peaceful and prosperous years of their domination. This phase came to an end with the beginning of Elizabethan influence.

Photographs

The photographs in this volume are by David H. Davison of PDI Photography, Dublin, with the following exceptions:
J. Banbury, *plate 80*
P. Collins, *plate 118*
Cooper & Co., *plate 243*
P. Harbison, *plates 3, 15, 35, 41, 95, 98, 104, 121, 171, 189, 200, 231-32, 252, 270, 338, 340*
J. Hunt, *plates 11, 21, 60, 67, 92, 116, 126, 190-91, 215, 217, 223-4, 226, 229, 233-34, 269, 314, 337, 339*
T. H. Mason, *plate 204*
R. J. Wiltshire, *plates 4, 30, 132, 236-42, 244-45, 253-59, 278, 297-98, 323-24, 330-31*

Period I: Knights

1 Timolin, Co. Kildare. Church of Ireland church. Effigy said to be that of Robert FitzRichard, Lord of Norragh. First half 13th century.
Catalogue number 91

2 Christchurch, Dublin city. On right the demi-figure of a knight—'Strongbow's son'.
Compare also pl. 17. 13th century (?).
Catalogue number 28

4 Hospital, Co. Limerick. Double effigy
of a knight and lady. Second half 13th
century.
Catalogue number 176

3 Hospital, Co. Limerick. Effigy
of a knight. c. 1260.
Catalogue number 175

6 St John's Priory, Kilkenny city. Knight's head as terminal of label moulding. c.1290. *Catalogue number 157*

5 Jerpoint, Co. Kilkenny. Incised slab of two unknown knights—'The Brethren'. Late 13th century. *Catalogue number 115*

7 Gowran, Co. Kilkenny. Effigy of a knight. 13th or early 14th century.
Catalogue number 103

8 Grey Abbey, Co. Down. Fragmentary effigy of a knight. Late 13th/early 14th century.
Catalogue number 24

9 Graiguenamanagh, Co.
Kilkenny. Effigy of an unknown
knight. Late 13th/early 14th
century.
Catalogue number 109

10 Ratoath, Co. Meath. Effigy of a knight.
Late 13th/early 14th century.
Catalogue number 201

11 Castlelost, Co. Westmeath. Effigy of a knight. 13th/14th century.
Catalogue number 259

12 Kilfane, Co. Kilkenny. Effigy of a Cantwell knight. c.1320.
Catalogue number 129

13 Kilfane, Co. Kilkenny. Effigy of a
Cantwell knight. c.1320. Detail. Compare
pl. 12.
Catalogue number 129

14 Cashel, Co. Tipperary. Church
of Ireland Cathedral of St John
the Baptist churchyard. Effigy
of a knight. First half 14th
century.
Catalogue number 230

15 Hospital, Co. Limerick. Flat effigy of a knight.
14th century (?).
Catalogue number 177

16 Dysert O'Dea, Co. Clare. Figure of a civilian.
14th century (?).
Catalogue number 4

17 Christchurch, Dublin city. Left, effigy of a knight—
'Strongbow's tomb'. c.1330. Compare also pl 2.
Catalogue number 32

Period I:
Civilian Ladies

19 New Ross, Co. Wexford. St. Mary's Church. Lower half of an effigy of a woman (?). First half 13th century.
Catalogue number 263

18 Christchurch, Dublin city. Effigy of a woman. Early 13th century.
Catalogue number 25

20 Christchurch, Dublin city. Effigy of a woman. 13th century.
Catalogue number 27

21 Kells, Co. Kilkenny. Fragmentary effigy of a woman.
13th century.
Catalogue number 127

22 Grey Abbey, Co. Down.
Effigy of a woman. Late 13th
century.
Catalogue number 23

23 Castledillon, Co. Kildare. Incised
figure of a woman. Recently removed to
St Wolstan's, Celbridge. Late 13th century.
Catalogue number 77

24 St Canice's, Kilkenny city. Label-stop
with the head of a woman. Late 13th
century.
Catalogue number 133

25 St Mary's parish church,
Kilkenny city. Effigy of Helen,
wife of William de Armayl. Late
13th/early 14th century.
Catalogue number 160

26 Cashel, Co. Tipperary. Church of Ireland Cathedral of St John the Baptist churchyard. Effigy of a woman. Late 13th/early 14th century.
Catalogue number 231

27 Cashel, Co. Tipperary. Church of Ireland Cathedral of St John the Baptist churchyard. Effigy of a Hackett lady. Late 13th/early 14th century.
Catalogue number 232

28 Cashel, Co. Tipperary. Church of Ireland Cathedral of St John the Baptist churchyard. Effigy of a woman. Late 13th/early 14th century.
Catalogue number 233

29 St Canice's, Kilkenny city. Incised figure of a woman.
Early 14th century.
Catalogue number 136

Period I:
Male/Female
Double Effigies

30 Athassel Priory, Co. Tipperary. Incised slab with a man and a woman. First half 14th century.
Catalogue number 222

31 and **32** Gowran, Co. Kilkenny. Effigies probably of (left) James le Butler and (right)
Eleanor de Bohun. c.1320–40.

Catalogue number 104   *Catalogue number 105*

33 Kells, Co. Meath. Double tomb-slab with Crucifixion. Second quarter 14th century.
Catalogue number 188

Period I:
Civilian Males

35 Gowran, Co. Kilkenny. Fragments of a head from an effigy of a civilian. Late 13th century.
Catalogue number 102

34 Youghal, Co. Cork. St Mary's Church. Composite effigy (head male; body female). Late 13th century.
Catalogue number 15

37 Cashel, Co. Tipperary. Presentation Convent. Effigy of a layman from the medieval church of St John the Baptist. Late 13th century.
Catalogue number 234

36 Thomastown, Co. Kilkenny. Effigy of a civilian. Late 13th century.
Catalogue number 168

38 Waterford Cathedral, Co. Waterford. Fragment of an effigy of a civilian. Late 13th century. *Catalogue number 253*

39 New Ross, Co. Wexford. St. Mary's Church. The 'Bambino' Stone. Late 13th century. *Catalogue number 266*

40 New Ross, Co. Wexford. St. Mary's Church. Effigy of a layman. Late 13th century. *Catalogue number 267*

41 Castleinch or Inchyologhan, Co. Kilkenny. Effigy of a male civilian. Late 13th/early 14th century.
Catalogue number 95a

42 Roscommon 'Abbey', Co. Roscommon. Effigy said to be that of Felim O'Connor. c.1300.
Catalogue number 212

43 Corcomroe, Co. Clare. Effigy
said to be that of King Conor na
Siudaine O'Brien. c.1300.
Catalogue number 3

44 New Ross, Co.Wexford.
St Mary's Church. Effigy of
Roger the Clerk. c.1300.
Catalogue number 272

45 New Ross, Co. Wexford. St Mary's Church. Effigy of a layman. c.1300.
Catalogue number 273

46 Athassel Priory, Co. Tipperary. Effigy of a nobleman, Walter or Richard de Burgo (?). Late 13th/early 14th century. At right, the small figure of a saint or prior for which see also pl. 84.
Catalogue number 219

47 Ballyhea, Co. Cork. Effigy of a
civilian. Early 14th century.
Catalogue number 13

48 Youghal, Co. Cork. St Mary's
Church. Effigy of Thomas Paris.
Early 14th century.
Catalogue number 17

49 Youghal, Co. Cork. St Mary's Church. Matheu le Mercer. Early 14th century.
Catalogue number 18

50 St Audoen's, Dublin city. Male effigy. Early 14th century.
Catalogue number 40

51 Callan, Co. Kilkenny. St
Mary's church. Effigy of a layman
(?). Early 14th century (?).
Catalogue number 93

52 Jerpoint, Co. Kilkenny. Effigy of
Thomas, a civilian. First half 14th century.
Catalogue number 119

53 St Mary's parish church,
Kilkenny city. Effigy of a man.
Second quarter 14th century.
Catalogue number 162

54 St Canice's, Kilkenny city. Incised slab
with fragmentary figure of a man (possibly
an ecclesiastic). 14th century.
Catalogue number 139

55 St Francis's Friary, Kilkenny
city. Corbel figure under vaulting
of tower. c.1347.
Catalogue number 156

56 St Francis's Friary, Kilkenny
city. Corbel figure under vaulting
of tower. c.1347.
Catalogue number 156

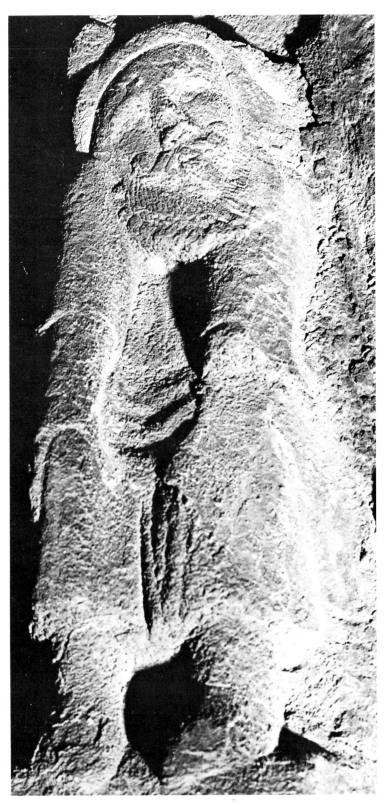

57 St Francis's Friary, Kilkenny city. Corbel
figure under vaulting of tower. c.1347.
Catalogue number 156

58 St Francis's Friary, Kilkenny
city. Corbel figure under vaulting
of tower. c.1347.
Catalogue number 156

59 St Francis's Friary, Kilkenny
city. Corbel figure under vaulting
of tower. c.1347
Catalogue number 156

Period I: Ecclesiastics

60 Slane, Co. Meath. Effigy of an
ecclesiastic formerly at Painestown, Co.
Meath. Late 12th/early 13th century.
Catalogue number 204

61 Jerpoint, Co. Kilkenny. Effigy of a
bishop (Felix O'Dullany? died 1202). Early
13th century.
Catalogue number 113

62 Christchurch, Dublin city.
Effigy of an archbishop, possibly
John Comyn (died 1212). Early
13th century.
Catalogue number 26

63 Newtown Trim, Co. Meath.
Effigy of an ecclesiastic (Simon de
Rochfort? died 1224). Early 13th
century.
Catalogue number 197

64 St Michan's, Dublin city.
Effigy of a bishop. First half 13th
century.
Catalogue number 42

65 Ferns, Co. Wexford. Effigy of a
bishop, probably John St John
(died 1243). Mid-13th century.
Catalogue number 262

66 St Mary's Cathedral, Limerick city. Effigy of a bishop
(13th century) under Bultingfort—Galwey canopied niche
(c.1500) in south aisle.
Catalogue number 178

67 Boyle Abbey, Co.
Roscommon. Tapering slab with
a crosier. 13th century.
Catalogue number 211

69 Kildare, Co. Kildare. Cathedral. Effigy
of a bishop, possibly John of Taunton
(1235-58).
Catalogue number 87

68 Gowran, Co. Kilkenny. Right,
effigy of Radoulfus, died 1253;
left, miniature effigy of a man
(heart-burial?). Mid-13th century.
Catalogue number 100
Catalogue number 99

70 Kildare, Co. Kildare. Cathedral. Effigy of a bishop, possibly John of Taunton.
Detail. Compare pl. 69.
Catalogue number 87

71 St Patrick's, Dublin city.
Effigy of a priest or deacon. 13th
century.
Catalogue number 43

72 Jerpoint, Co. Kilkenny. Effigy
of a bishop, said to be William of
Cork. c.1266(?).
Catalogue number 114

74 Corcomroe, Co. Clare. Effigy of a bishop. 13th century.
Catalogue number 2

73 St Patrick's. Dublin city. De Saundford effigy. Second half 13th century.
Catalogue number 46

75 Ardfert, Co. Kerry. Cathedral.
Effigy of an abbot or a bishop.
Late 13th century.
Catalogue number 70

76 Ardfert, Co. Kerry. Cathedral. Effigy of
an abbot. Late 13th/early 14th century.
Catalogue number 69

78 Kilfenora, Co. Clare. Cathedral. Head of a bishop over
traceried niche in the ruined chancel. Early 14th century.
Catalogue number 7

7 Kilfenora, Co. Clare.
Cathedral. Incised slab of a bishop
showing Irish form of crosier.
Late 13th/early 14th century.
Catalogue number 10

79 Kilfenora, Co. Clare. Cathedral. Mitred head and shoulders over the south doorway. 14th century.
Catalogue number 9

80 Ardfert, Co. Kerry. Franciscan Friary. Effigy of a bishop or abbot. Early 14th century.
Catalogue number 71

82 Kildare, Co. Kildare. Cathedral. Effigy of a bishop (formerly at Religeen). Early 14th century.
Catalogue number 88

81 St Patrick's, Dublin city. 'St Patrick' —composite figure. Body, c.1300; head, 17th century.
Catalogue number 47

83 Newtown Jerpoint churchyard, Co. Kilkenny. Effigy of an ecclesiastic. Early 14th century.
Catalogue number 165

84 Athassel Priory, Co. Tipperary. Small figure of a saint or prior. First half 14th century. Compare also pl. 46.
Catalogue number 221

85 Inistioge, Co. Kilkenny. Church of Ireland church. Incised figure of a prior. First half 14th century.
Catalogue number 110

86 Jerpoint, Co. Kilkenny. Fragment of an incised slab. First half 14th century.
Catalogue number 118

87 Jerpoint, Co. Kilkenny. Incised figure of an abbot(?). First half 14th century.
Catalogue number 117

88 Kilfenora, Co. Clare. Cathedral. Effigy of a bishop in the ruined chancel. First half 14th century.
Catalogue number 11

89 St Canice's, Kilkenny city. Incised fragment showing an ecclesiastic. 14th century. *Catalogue number 137*

90 St Canice's, Kilkenny city. Incised slab with
fragmentary figure of an ecclesiastic. 14th century.
Catalogue number 138

91 Skreen, Co. Meath. Miniature effigy of
a bishop. 14th century.
Catalogue number 202

Period I:
Head–Slabs
Civilian Ladies

92 *Left, upper*. Dungarvan, Co. Kilkenny. Head-slab of a woman. 13th century.
Catalogue number 96

93 *Left, lower*. Black Abbey, Kilkenny city. Head-slab of a woman. 13th century.
Catalogue number 130

94 *Right*. St Mary's parish church, Kilkenny city. Coffin-shaped slab with the head of a woman. Probably 13th century.
Catalogue number 159

95 New Ross, Co. Wexford. St Mary's Church. Head-
slab of Isabel. 13th century.
Catalogue number 264

96 New Ross, Co. Wexford. St Mary's Church. Head-slab of Alis la Kerdif. Late 13th century.
Catalogue number 268

97 New Ross, Co. Wexford. St Mary's Church. Head-slab of a woman(?). Late 13th/early 14th century.
Catalogue number 269

Period I:
Double Head-Slabs
Male and Female
Civilians

98 Bannow, Co.Wexford. Double
head–slab. Late 13th century.
Catalogue number 260

99 Christchurch, Dublin city. Fragment of a double head-slab. c.1300.
Catalogue number 30

100 Trim, Co. Meath. St
Patrick's Church. Double
head-slab with Crucifixion.
Second quarter of 14th century.
Catalogue number 209

Period I:
Head-Slabs
Civilian Males

101 New Ross, Co. Wexford. St Mary's Church. Head-slab of a man. 13th century.
Catalogue number 265

102 Youghal, Co. Cork. St Mary's Church. Head-slab of a man named Alun. Late 13th century.
Catalogue number 16

103 Cashel, Co. Tipperary. Presentation Convent. Head-slab of a man. Late 13th century.
Catalogue number 235

104 Tullylease, Co. Cork. Cross-slab with part of an incised figure. Late 13th/early 14th century.
Catalogue number 13a

105 Christchurch, Dublin city. Head-slab
of a man. c.1300.
Catalogue number 29

106 St Selskar's, Wexford town. Head-slab with a ship. c.1300.
Catalogue number 275

107 St Canice's, Kilkenny city. Head-slab of a man. Early 14th century.
Catalogue number 135

Period I:
Head-Slabs
Ecclesiastics

108 Gowran, Co. Kilkenny.
Head-slab of an ecclesiastic. 13th
century.
Catalogue number 101

109 Jerpoint, Co. Kilkenny.
Incised head-slab of an
ecclesiastic. Late 13th/early 14th
century.
Catalogue number 116

110 St Canice's, Kilkenny city. Head-slab of a (?) priest or (?) layman in sunken reserve.
Late 13th/early 14th century.
Catalogue number 134

Hiatus

111 Ballykeefe, Co. Kilkenny.
Figure of a woman. c.1340-60.
Catalogue number 92

112 St Canice's, Kilkenny city.
Effigy of Bishop de Ledrede.
c.1361.
Catalogue number 140

113 Kentstown, Co. Meath.
Effigy of Sir Thomas de Tuite.
1363.
Catalogue number 189

114 St Mary's parish church, Kilkenny
city. Effigies of William Goer and his wife
Margaret. Second half 14th century.
Catalogue number 161

116 Slane Castle, Co. Meath.
Effigy of a bishop or abbot. Late
14th/early 15th century.
Catalogue number 206

115 Knocktopher, Co. Kilkenny. Double
effigy of a man and woman. Second half
14th century.
Catalogue number 164

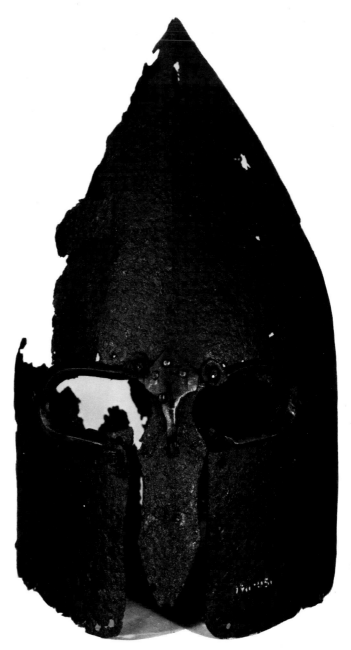

118 Lough Henney, Co. Down. Barbut.
c.1380. See Vol. 1, pp. 54 and 178.

117 Jerpoint, Co. Kilkenny. Cloister
arcade. Knight. c.1400.
Catalogue number 124

119 Jerpoint, Co. Kilkenny. Cloister arcade. Fragment of knight. c.1400.
Catalogue number 125a

120 Jerpoint, Co. Kilkenny. Cloister arcade. Fragment of knight. c.1400.
Catalogue number 125b

121 Jerpoint, Co. Kilkenny. Cloister
arcade. Fragments of knights, one with a
sword.
Catalogue number 125c

122 Jerpoint, Co. Kilkenny. Cloister
arcade. Figure of a woman. c.1400.
Catalogue number 125d

124 Jerpoint, Co. Kilkenny. Cloister
arcade. Head of a knight. c.1400.
Catalogue number 125e

123 Newtown, Jerpoint, Co. Kilkenny. Figure of a woman. Originally from the cloister arcade at Jerpoint.
Catalogue number 125d

125 Jerpoint, Co. Kilkenny. Cloister arcade. Mitred head.
c.1400.
Catalogue number 125f

126 Carrickbeg church, Co. Tipperary. Capital with heads of females and of a bishop. c.1336.
Catalogue number 223

127 Jerpoint, Co. Kilkenny. Cloister arcade. Figure of a
hooded layman in cape. c.1400.
Catalogue number 125g

128 Jerpoint, Co. Kilkenny. Cloister
arcade. Figure of a layman with tunic.
c.1400.
Catalogue number 125h

129 Jerpoint, Co. Kilkenny. Cloister
arcade. Figure of a bishop or abbot. c.1400.
Catalogue number 125i

130 Jerpoint, Co. Kilkenny. Cloister arcade.
Figure of a monk—St Dominic(?). c.1400.
Catalogue number 125j

131 Jerpoint, Co. Kilkenny. Cloister arcade.
Figure of St Margaret. c.1400.
Catalogue number 125k

132 Kilfenora, Co. Clare. Cathedral.
Effigy of a cleric in the ruined chancel.
Early 15th century (?).
Catalogue Number 12

133 Skreen, Co. Meath. Head-
slab of a man. First quarter 15th
century.
Catalogue number 203

Period II:
Knights
including Double Effigies

134 Killeen, Co. Meath. Tomb of a Plunket knight and his wife. Mid-15th century.
Catalogue number 190a

135 Killeen, Co. Meath. Effigy
of knight. Mid-15th century.
Catalogue number 191

136 Killeen, Co. Meath. Tomb of a Plunket knight and
his wife. Mid-15th century.
Catalogue number 194

137 Howth, Co. Dublin. St Mary's 'Abbey'. Effigies of
Christopher St Lawrence and his wife Anne Plunket.
c.1462.
Catalogue number 50a

138 Dunsany, Co. Meath. Effigies of a Plunket knight
and his wife. c.1463-72.
Catalogue number 187a

139 Rathmore, Co. Meath. Tomb of Sir Thomas
Plunket and his wife Marion Cruise. c. 1471.
Catalogue number 200a

140 St Audoen's, Dublin city. Tomb of Roland FitzEustace, Baron of Portlester, and his wife Margaret Jenico. 1482.
Catalogue number 41

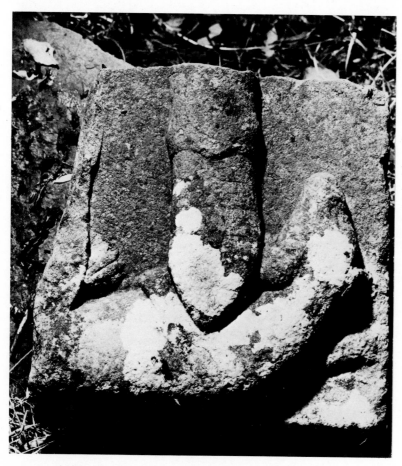

141 Castletown, Co. Meath. Kilpatrick church. Fragment of the effigy of a knight, possibly from a double tomb. Late 15th century.
Catalogue number 184a

142 Ballymore Eustace, Co. Kildare. Church of Ireland church. Effigy of a FitzEustace knight. Early 16th century. *Catalogue number 76*

143 Lusk, Co. Dublin. Church of Ireland church. Effigy
of James Bermingham. 1637.
Catalogue number 52

144 New Abbey. Kilcullen, Co. Kildare. Effigies of
Roland FitzEustace, Baron of Portlester, and his wife
Margaret Janico. c.1496.
Catalogue number 81a

145 StWerburgh's, Dublin city. Purcell double tomb, 1500–20.
Catalogue number 49

146 Stamullen, Co. Meath. Tomb of a (?) Preston knight
and his wife. c.1540.
Catalogue number 207

147 Dunfierth, Co. Kildare. Effigy of
Walter Bermingham. c.1548.
Catalogue number 80a

148 Castlemartin, Co. Kildare. Castle-
martin House. Fragmentary effigy of a
FitzEustace knight. Early 16th century.
Catalogue number 78a

149 Athboy, Co. Meath. Double tomb of a knight and
lady. Early 16th century.
Catalogue number 182a

150 St Canice's, Kilkenny city. Effigy of
James Schorthals. 1507.
Catalogue number 141a

151 Kilcooley Abbey, Co. Tipperary.
Effigy of Pierce FitzOge Butler. c.1526.
Catalogue number 243a

152 Fertagh, Co. Kilkenny. Effigies of a MacGillapatrick knight and his wife. 1510-40.
Catalogue number 98a

153 St Canice's, Kilkenny city.
Effigy of John Grace. 1552.
Catalogue number 145a

154 St Canice's, Kilkenny city. Tomb of
Richard Butler, Viscount Mountgarret.
1571.
Catalogue number 146a

155 St John's Priory, Kilkenny city. Double Purcell
tomb. 16th century.
Catalogue number 158a

157 National Museum of Ireland, Dublin.
Part of a recumbent effigy of a knight.
Early 16th century.
Catalogue number 35

156 Abbeyleix, Co. Laois.
Abbey Leix House. Effigy of
Malachy MacOwny O'More.
1502.
Catalogue number 170

158 St Canice's, Kilkenny city. Effigies of Piers Butler, 8th Earl of Ormond, and his wife Margaret FitzGerald. c.1539.
Catalogue number 142a–b

159 St Canice's, Kilkenny city. Effigy of Piers Butler,
8th Earl of Ormond. c.1539. Detail.
Catalogue number 142a

160 St Canice's, Kilkenny city. Effigy of Margaret
FitzGerald, wife of Piers Butler, 8th Earl of Ormond.
c.1539. Detail.
Catalogue number 142b

161 Gowran, Co. Kilkenny. Effigy of Butler knight.
First half 16th century.
Catalogue number 107a

162 Gowran, Co. Kilkenny. Effigies of two Butler knights.
First half 16th century.
Catalogue number 108a

163 Waterford Cathedral, Co. Waterford.
Effigy of an unknown knight. First half
16th century.
Catalogue number 256a

164 St Canice's, Kilkenny city. Effigy of
(?) James Butler, 9th Earl of Ormond.
c.1546(?).
Catalogue number 143a

165 St Canice's. Kilkenny city. Tomb-slab of Edmund
Purcell. c.1549.
Catalogue number 144

166 Thurles, Co. Tipperary. Church of Ireland church.
Effigies of Edmund Archer (?) and his wife. c.1520.
Catalogue number 246a

167 Clonmel, Co. Tipperary. Tomb of Thomas and Ellen Butler. 1530-40.
Catalogue number 236a–b

168 Dungiven, Co. Derry.
Cahan or St Mary's Abbey.
'O'Cahan' tomb. Effigy of a
knight popularly identified as
Cooey na nGall O'Cahan. Last
quarter 15th century.
Catalogue number 20a

169 Glinsk, Co. Galway. Ballynakill
church. Effigy of a Burke knight. First
quarter 16th century.
Catalogue number 66

170 Shantallow, Co. Derry. Fragmentary effigy of an unknown knight. c.1560-70.
Catalogue number 21

171 Sligo Abbey, Co. Sligo.
Slab of Donat O'Suibne, 1577 (?).
Catalogue number 218

Period II:
Civilian Ladies

172 Malahide, Co. Dublin. Church in the grounds of
Malahide Castle. Effigy said to be that of Maud Plunket.
Mid-15th century.
Catalogue number 54a

173 Castletown, Co. Meath. Kilpatrick church. Fragment
of an effigy of a woman, possibly from a double tomb.
Late 15th century.
Catalogue number 184

174 Callan, Co. Kilkenny. St Mary's Church. Architectural head of a lady. Early 16th century.
Catalogue number 95

175 National Museum of Ireland, Dublin. Fragment of the effigy of a woman.
Mid-16th century.
Catalogue number 36

176 St Canice's, Kilkenny city. Effigy of Honorina Grace. Probably before 1596. *Catalogue number 148a*

177 Gowran, Co. Kilkenny. Effigy of a woman. Early 16th century. *Catalogue number 106*

178 Black Abbey, Kilkenny city. Effigy of
a woman. First half 16th century.
Catalogue number 131

179 St Canice's, Kilkenny city. Effigy of an
unknown woman. First half 16th century.
Catalogue number 147a

180 Waterford Cathedral, Co. Waterford. Fragmentary
effigy of a woman. First half 16th century.
Catalogue number 257

Period II:
Double Civilian Effigy
Civilian Males
Ecclesiastics

181 Jerpoint, Co. Kilkenny. Effigies of a harper and his wife. Early 16th century.
Catalogue number 120

182 Toomevara, Co. Tipperary. Tomb-
stone with figure of an O'Mara. Late
15th century(?).
Catalogue number 248

183 Killeen, Co. Meath. Effigy of a bishop.
Second half 15th century.
Catalogue number 193

184 Kilcooley Abbey, Co. Tipperary.
Floor-slab of Abbot Philip O'Molwanayn.
1463.
Catalogue number 242

185 St Patrick's, Dublin city. Effigy of Archbishop
Tregury. 1471 or later.
Catalogue number 48

186 Kildare, Co. Kildare. Cathedral. Effigy of Bishop Walter Wellesly. (Formerly at Great Connell). c.1539.
Catalogue number 89a

187 Cashel, Co. Tipperary. St Patrick's Cathedral. Fragmentary effigy of an archbishop. 16th century(?).
Catalogue number 229

Period I:
Tomb Surrounds
1200-1350

188 Athassel Priory, Co. Tipperary. Tomb-front with knights. Late 13th/early 14th century.
Catalogue number 220

Hiatus:
Tomb Surrounds
1350-1450

189 Tralee, Co. Kerry.
Dominican Priory garden. Figure
of a knight or gallowglass from
a tomb-chest (?). 14th/15th
century.
Catalogue number 75

190 Slane, Co. Meath. West end of 'Apostle Tomb' at St Erc's Hermitage. Late 14th/
early 15th century.
Catalogue number 205a

191a-191b Slane, Co. Meath. 'Apostle Tomb' at St. Erc's Hermitage. Late 14th/early 15th century.
Catalogue number 205b

Period II:
Tomb Surrounds
1450-1570

192 Howth, Co. Dublin. St Mary's 'Abbey'. St Lawrence tomb. Eastern end-panel.
c.1462.
Catalogue number 50b

193 Howth, Co. Dublin. St Mary's 'Abbey', St Lawrence tomb. Western end-panel.
c.1462.
Catalogue number 50c

194 Dunsany, Co. Meath. Double Plunket tomb. Eastern end-slab of the tomb-chest.
c.1463-72. Detail.
Catalogue number 187b

195 Dunsany, Co. Meath. Double Plunket tomb. Western end-slab of the tomb-chest.
c.1463-72.
Catalogue number 187c

196 Rathmore, Co. Meath. The southern end-slab of the tomb-chest of the double Plunket tomb. c.1471.
Catalogue number 200c

197 Rathmore, Co. Meath. The north end of the tomb-chest of the double Plunket tomb. c.1471.
Catalogue number 200d

198 Duleek, Co. Meath. Tomb-chest of Preston/Plunket tomb. East end. Second half
15th century.
Catalogue number 186c

199 Duleek, Co. Meath. Tomb-chest of Preston/Plunket tomb. West end. Second half
15th century.
Catalogue number 186d

200 Newtown Trim, Co. Meath. Apex of niche-head showing the Coronation of the Virgin and a head between two eagles. Late 15th century.
Catalogue number 198

201 New Abbey, Kilcullen, Co. Kildare. FitzEustace, Baron of Portlester, tomb. Side of tomb-chest. c.1496.
Catalogue number 81b

202 New Abbey, Kilcullen, Co. Kildare.
FitzEustace, Baron of Portlester, tomb.
End of tomb-chest showing St Michael.
c.1496.
Catalogue number 81c

203 Christchurch, Dublin city. Composite figure under a
niche in the crypt. c. 1 500.
Catalogue number 33

204 St Werburgh's, Dublin city. Original northern side-panel of Purcell double tomb. 1500–20.
Catalogue number 49b

205 St Werburgh's, Dublin city. East end of northern side-panel. 1500–20.
Catalogue number 49b–c

206 St Werburgh's, Dublin city. Eastern end-panel. 1500-20.
Catalogue number 49d

207 St Werburgh's, Dublin city. Western end-panel. 1500-20.
Catalogue number 49e

208 Castlemartin, Co. Kildare. Castlemartin House. FitzEustace tomb. Fragments of end-slabs of tomb-chest. Early 16th century.
Catalogue number 78b

209 Castlemartin, Co. Kildare. Castlemartin House. FitzEustace tomb. Fragments of side-panels of tomb-chest. Early 16th century.

210 Castlemartin, Co. Kildare. Castlemartin House. FitzEustace tomb. Fragments of side-panels of tomb-chest. Early 16th century.
Catalogue number 78c

211 Castlemartin, Co. Kildare. Castlemartin House. FitzEustace tomb. Detail of animals on plinth. Early 16th century.
Catalogue number 78d

212 Athboy, Co. Meath. Dexter front-slab.
Original end of tomb-chest of double tomb.
Early 16th century.
Catalogue number 182b

213 Athboy, Co. Meath. Sinister front-slab. Original head end of tomb-chest of double tomb. Early 16th century.
Catalogue number 182c

215 Athlone, Co. Westmeath. Figure of a woman formerly at St Mary's Catholic church. 16th century. (From an old photograph.)
Catalogue number 258

214 Ballinabrackey, Co. Meath. Fragments of tomb-chest in the Catholic church. Early 16th century.
Catalogue number 183

216 New Abbey, Kilcullen, Co. Kildare. Part of a tomb-chest carved with four figures of saints. First half 16th century.
Catalogue number 82

217 Kildare, Co. Kildare. Carmelite Priory. St Michael or St Gabriel (?). Early 16th century.
Catalogue number 85

218 Kildare, Co. Kildare. Cathedral. Wellesly tomb (formerly at Great Connell).
Head end-slab showing *Ecce Homo*. c.1539.
Catalogue number 89b

219 Kildare, Co. Kildare. Cathedral. Wellesly tomb (formerly at Great Connell). Foot
end-slab showing Crucifixion. c.1539.
Catalogue number 89c

220 Kildare, Co. Kildare. Cathedral. Wellesly tomb (formerly at Great Connell).
Fragment of western side-panel of tomb-chest showing St Patrick and St John the
Evangelist. c.1539.
Catalogue number 89d

221 Kildare, Co. Kildare. Cathedral. Wellesly tomb.
Fragment of tomb-chest showing St Peter. Formerly at
Great Connell. c.1539.
Catalogue number 89d

222 Kildare, Co. Kildare. Cathedral.
Upper fragment of a figure of St Andrew
now serving as part of eastern long-side
of the tomb-chest of the Wellesly tomb.
(Formerly at Great Connell). Mid-16th
century.

224 Kildare, Co. Kildare. Cathedral. Figure of St
Thaddeus at present part of the eastern long-side
of the tomb-chest of the Wellesly tomb.
Mid-16th century.
Catalogue number 89e

223 Kildare, Co. Kildare. Cathedral.
Lower fragment of a figure of St Andrew
at present serving as part of the eastern
long-side of the tomb-chest of the Wellesly
tomb. (Formerly at Great Connell).
Mid-16th century.
Catalogue number 89e

225 Kildare, Co. Kildare. Cathedral.
Fragment of a figure of St Matthias serving
as part of the eastern long-side of the
tomb-chest of the Wellesly tomb. (Formerly
at Great Connell). Mid-16th century.
Catalogue number 89e

226 Kildare, Co. Kildare.
Cathedral. End-return now
forming part of the eastern side-
panel of the tomb-chest of the
Wellesly tomb. (Formerly at
Great Connell). Mid-16th century.
Catalogue number 89e

227 Dunfierth, Co. Kildare. Bermingham tomb. Tomb-chest, south side. c.1548.
Catalogue number 80b

228 Dunfierth, Co. Kildare. Bermingham tomb. Tomb-chest, north side. c.1548.
Catalogue number 80c

229 Dunfierth, Co. Kildare. Bermingham tomb. Tomb-chest. Fragment of head of St James Major now on the sinister side of the effigy. c.1548.
Catalogue number 80c

231 Dunfierth, Co. Kildare. Bermingham tomb. Fragment of tomb-chest—head of Christ (from foot end-panel) now on dexter side of the effigy. c.1548.
Catalogue number 80e

230 Dunfierth, Co. Kildare. Bermingham tomb. End-slab showing Crucifixion. c.1548.
Catalogue number 80d

232 Kildare, Co. Kildare. Cathedral. Fragments of a tomb-chest. Second half 16th century.
Catalogue number 90

233 Kildare, Co. Kildare. Carmelite Priory.
Crucifixion from a tomb–chest. Second half 16th century.
Catalogue number 83

234 Kildare, Co. Kildare. Carmelite Priory. *Ecce Homo*
from a tomb-chest. Second half 16th century.
Catalogue number 84

235 Ennis, Co. Clare. Friary. The Creagh tomb (1843) incorporating panels from the MacMahon tomb, and from another tomb.
Catalogue number 5a

236 Ennis, Co. Clare. Friary.
Creagh tomb, west end, archbishop from MacMahon tomb.
c.1470.
Catalogue number 5b1

237 Ennis, Co. Clare. Friary. Creagh tomb, west end, The Betrayal of Christ. c.1470. *Catalogue number 5b2*

238 Ennis, Co. Clare. Friary. Creagh tomb, south side, The Flagellation of Christ.
c.1470.
Catalogue number 5c1

239 Ennis, Co. Clare. Friary. Creagh tomb, south side, The Crucifixion. c.1470.
Catalogue number 5c2

240 Ennis, Co. Clare. Friary. Creagh tomb, south side, The Entombment of Christ.
c.1470.
Catalogue number 5c3

241 Ennis, Co. Clare. Friary. Creagh tomb, east end, The Resurrection of Christ.
c.1470.
Catalogue number 5d1

242 Ennis, Co. Clare. Friary. Creagh tomb, east end, a
female figure (Holy Wisdom?). c.1470.
Catalogue number 5d2

243 English Nottingham alabasters. The Entombment and Resurrection. 1420–60.
Compare catalogue numbers 5c3 and 5d1

244 Ennis, Co. Clare. Friary. Creagh tomb. Christ and Apostles above mensa. c.1470.
Catalogue number 5f

245 Ennis, Co. Clare. Friary. Creagh tomb. Apostles above mensa.
Catalogue number 5f

246 Ennis, Co. Clare. Friary. Figure of archbishop on
canopied tomb of Western type—at present under the
tower. Second half 15th century.
Catalogue number 6a

247 Ennis, Co. Clare. Friary. Virgin and Child on
canopied tomb of Western type—at present under the
tower. Second half 15th century.
Catalogue number 6b

248 Dungiven, Co. Derry. Cahan or St Mary's Abbey. 'O'Cahan' tomb. Last quarter 15th century.
Catalogue number 20b

249 Dungiven, Co. Derry. Cahan or St Mary's Abbey.
'O'Cahan' tomb. Figure of a gallowglass on tomb-front.
Last quarter 15th century.
Catalogue number 20b

250 Roscommon 'Abbey', Co. Roscommon. Tomb-front below figure of Felim O'Connor, with figures of gallowglasses. Late 15th century.
Catalogue number 213

252 Roscommon 'Abbey', Co. Roscommon. Fragment of a tomb-front with two niches and part of a figure. Late 15th century.
Catalogue number 214

251 Roscommon 'Abbey', Co. Roscommon. Detail of tomb-front—(pl. 250) under effigy of Felim O'Connor. Late 15th century.
Catalogue number 213

253 Strade, Co. Mayo. Canopied tomb with double front slab. Second half 15th century.
Catalogue number 180a–b

254 Strade, Co. Mayo. The dexter slab of the canopied tomb. Second half 15th century.
Catalogue number 180a

255 Strade, Co. Mayo. The sinister slab of the canopied tomb. Second half 15th century. *Catalogue number 180b*

256 Strade, Co. Mayo. Tomb-frontal or altar reredos. Second half 15th century. *Catalogue number 181*

259 Kilconnell, Co. Galway. Franciscan Friary. Canopied tomb. Detail of finial. Second half 15th century.
Catalogue number 67b

257 Kilconnell, Co. Galway. Franciscan Friary. Canopied tomb. Second half 15th century.
Catalogue number 67a–b

258 Kilconnell, Co. Galway. Franciscan Friary. Canopied tomb. Detail showing St John and St James Major. Second half 15th century. *Catalogue number 67a*

260 St Nicholas, Galway city. The Joyce tomb. Late 15th
century.
Catalogue number 63

261 St Nicholas, Galway city. The Joyce tomb. Detail of
Christ as Judge. Late 15th century.
Catalogue number 63

262 St Nicholas, Galway city. Corbel supported by an angle. 15th century.
Catalogue number 65

263 St Nicholas, Galway city. Sculptured corbel showing
Joshua with grapes. 15th century.
Catalogue number 65

264 Athenry, Co. Galway. Dominican Priory. Angle-shaft, probably from a gabled tomb of Western type. Late 15th/early 16th century.
Catalogue number 62

265 Athenry, Co. Galway. The Dominican Priory.
Gabled tomb of Western type showing also fragment
of tomb-front with an angel. Early 16th century.
Catalogue numbers 58, 60

266 Athenry, Co. Galway. The Dominican Priory.
Gabled tomb of Western type. Detail of Virgin and
Child. Early 16th century.
Catalogue number 58

267 St Nicholas, Galway city. The Archer
tomb. Detail showing an angel. First half
16th century.
Catalogue number 64

268 Sligo Abbey, Co. Sligo. The O'Craian canopied tomb. The tomb-front. 1506.
Catalogue number 217

269 Askeaton Friary, Co.
Limerick. Fragment of a tomb-
chest. First half 16th century.
Catalogue number 173

270 Askeaton Friary, Co.
Limerick. Fragment of a tomb-
front with figure of a bishop.
16th century.
Catalogue number 174

271 Waterford Cathedral, Co. Waterford. Tomb of James Rice. The south side. After 1487.
Catalogue number 255b

272 Waterford Cathedral, Co. Waterford. Tomb of James Rice. The east end. After 1487.
Catalogue number 255c

273 Waterford Cathedral, Co. Waterford. Tomb of James Rice. The west end. After 1487.
Catalogue number 255e

274 Jerpoint, Co. Kilkenny. South side of altar-tomb of Walter Brenach and Katherine Poher. 1501.
Catalogue number 123a

275 Jerpoint, Co. Kilkenny. Crucifixion at west end of altar-tomb of Walter Brenach and Katherine Poher. 1501.
Catalogue number 123c

276 Fertagh, Co. Kilkenny. MacGillapatrick double tomb. Tomb-surround. 1510-40. *Catalogue number 98b*

277 Fertagh, Co. Kilkenny. MacGillapatrick double tomb. Tomb-surround. 1510-40. *Catalogue number 98b*

278 Kilcooley Abbey, Co. Tipperary. Side-slabs of tomb-chest of Pierce FitzOge Butler. c.1526.
Catalogue number 243b

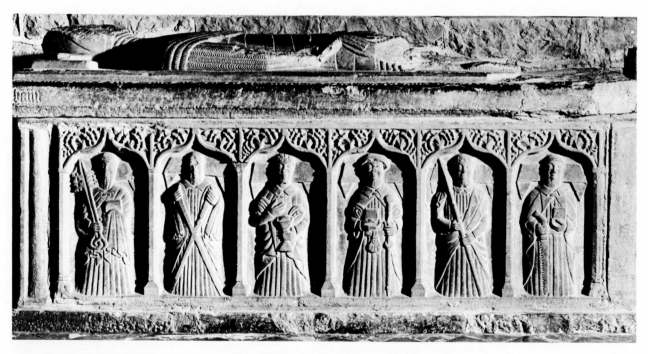

279 St Canice's, Kilkenny city. Tomb of John Grace. Tomb-front. 1552.
Catalogue number 145b

280 St Canice's, Kilkenny city. Tomb of John Grace. Head end of tomb-chest and signature of Rory O'Tunney. 1552.
Catalogue number 145c

281 St Canice's, Kilkenny city. Tomb of John Grace. Foot end of tomb–chest. The Grace arms.
Catalogue number 145d

282 St Canice's, Kilkenny city. Crucifixion at head end of tomb of Piers Butler, 8th Earl of Ormond, and his wife Margaret FitzGerald. 16th century.
Catalogue number 142c

283 St Canice's, Kilkenny city. Fragments of figures of Apostles at the west end of the north aisle, and originally under the Schorthals tomb. 16th century.
Catalogue number 151

284 St Canice's, Kilkenny city. Fragment of a tomb-front against the wall of the north aisle, originally under the Schorthals effigy. 16th century.
Catalogue number 150

285 St Canice's, Kilkenny city. Christ bound to the Column and the Instruments of the Passion from the south side-panel of the tomb-chest at present supporting the effigies of Piers Butler, 8th Earl of Ormond and his wife, Margaret FitzGerald. (See also pl. 286). 16th century.

Catalogue number 142f

286 St Canice's, Kilkenny city. Crucifixion on south side of tomb-chest supporting effigies of Piers Butler, 8th Earl of Ormond and his wife Margaret FitzGerald. (See also pl. 285). 16th century.
Catalogue number 142f

287 Cashel, Co. Tipperary. St Patrick's Cathedral. Front of tomb-chest. 16th century.
Catalogue number 228

288 St Mary's parish church, Kilkenny city. Fragment of a
tomb-chest with figure of an archbishop. 16th century.
Catalogue number 163

289 St John's Priory, Kilkenny city. Double Purcell tomb. Front-slab of tomb-chest. 16th century.
Catalogue number 158b

290 St John's Priory, Kilkenny city. Double Purcell tomb. East end-slab of tomb-chest. 16th century.
Catalogue number 158c

291 St John's Priory, Kilkenny city. Double Purcell tomb. West end-slab of tomb-chest.
16th century.
Catalogue number 158d

292 St Canice's, Kilkenny city. Tomb of Honorina Grace. Side-panel of tomb-chest.
16th century.
Catalogue number 148b

293 Jerpoint, Co. Kilkenny. Side-panel; part of a tomb-chest. 16th century.
Catalogue number 122a

294 Jerpoint, Co. Kilkenny. End-panel; part of a tomb-chest. 16th century.
Catalogue number 122b

295 Jerpoint, Co. Kilkenny. Head-end of a tomb-chest. 16th century.
Catalogue number 121a

296 Jerpoint, Co. Kilkenny. Side-panel of a tomb-chest. 16th century.
Catalogue number 121b

297 Cashel, Co. Tipperary. St Patrick's Cathedral. Side-slab from a tomb-chest. Southern side. 16th century.
Catalogue number 226a

298 Cashel, Co. Tipperary. St. Patrick's Cathedral. Fragments of a side-slab from a tomb-chest. Northern side. 16th century.
Catalogue number 226b

299 St Canice's, Kilkenny city. Tomb of Richard Butler. Front of tomb-chest. 1571.
Catalogue number 146b

300 Kilcooley Abbey, Co. Tipperary. End-slab of tomb-chest with three saints.
Second half 16th century.
Catalogue number 244

301 Cashel, Co. Tipperary. St Patrick's Cathedral. End-slab of a tomb-chest in north
wall of south chapel in the north transept. Late 16th century.
Catalogue number 229a

302 St Canice's, Kilkenny city. Slab showing the Trinity
(from St Mary's, Kilkenny city). Late 16th century (?).
Catalogue number 152

303 Waterford Cathedral, Co. Waterford. Side-slab from tomb of unknown knight.
First half 16th century.
Catalogue number 256b

304 Gowran, Co. Kilkenny. Tomb of a Butler knight. South side showing Apostles.
First half 16th century.
Catalogue number 107b

305 Gowran, Co. Kilkenny. Tomb of a Butler knight. East end. First half 16th century.
Catalogue number 107c

306 Gowran, Co. Kilkenny. Tomb-front at present supporting the effigies of two Butler knights. First half 16th century.
Catalogue number 108b

307 Gowran, Co. Kilkenny. End-slab showing Crucifixion at present at foot-end of tomb-chest under the effigies of two Butler knights. First half 16th century.
Catalogue number 108d

308 St Canice's. Kilkenny city. Tomb-front under effigy of (?) James, 9th Earl of Ormond. First half 16th century.
Catalogue number 143b–c

309 St Canice's, Kilkenny city. Tomb-front under effigy of James Schorthals. First half 16th century.
Catalogue number 141b

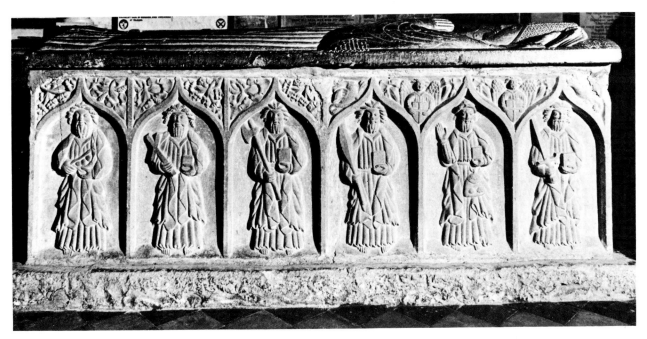

310 St Canice's, Kilkenny city. Northern side-panel under effigies of Piers Butler, 8th Earl of Ormond, and his wife Margaret FitzGerald. First half 16th century. *Catalogue number 142d*

311 St Canice's, Kilkenny city. Tomb of an unknown woman. Side-panel of tomb-chest. First half 16th century. *Catalogue number 147b*

312 St Canice's, Kilkenny city. Tomb of an unknown woman. East end of tomb-chest.
First half 16th century.
Catalogue number 147c

313 St Canice's, Kilkenny city. Tomb of an unknown woman. West end of tomb-chest. First half 16th century.
Catalogue number 147d

314 St Canice's, Kilkenny city. Fragment of tomb-front with two figures against the west wall of the north aisle. 16th century.
Catalogue number 153

315 St Canice's, Kilkenny city. Fragment of tomb-chest
in east gable of the sexton's house. Female saint. 16th
century.
Catalogue number 154

316 St Canice's, Kilkenny city. Fragment of tomb-chest
in east gable of the sexton's house. An abbess. 16th century.
Catalogue number 154

317 St Canice's, Kilkenny city. Fragment of tomb-chest in east gable of the sexton's house. St Gabriel. 16th century. *Catalogue number 154*

318 St Canice's, Kilkenny city. Fragment of tomb-chest in east gable of the sexton's house. Female saint. 16th century.
Catalogue number 154

319 St Canice's, Kilkenny city. Fragments of a tomb-chest
beneath tomb-niche at the north end of the north transept.
16th century.
Catalogue number 149

320 Kilboy, Co. Tipperary. Fragment of a tomb-chest with *Pietà* near Kilboy Holy
Well. Early 16th century.
Catalogue number 241

321 Callan, Co. Kilkenny. St. Mary's Church. Fragment of a tomb-chest panel showing St Catherine. 16th century.
Catalogue number 94

322 Piltown, Co. Kilkenny. Catholic graveyard. Panel
from a tomb-chest with the Virgin and Child. 16th century.
Catalogue number 166

323 Cashel, Co. Tipperary. St Patrick's Cathedral. Side-slab from a tomb-chest. North side. First half 16th century.
Catalogue number 227a

324 Cashel, Co. Tipperary. St Patrick's Cathedral. Side-slab from a tomb-chest. South side. First half 16th century.
Catalogue number 227b

325 Cashel, Co. Tipperary. St Patrick's Cathedral. End-slab (?) of a tomb-chest. First half 16th century.
Catalogue number 225

326 Thurles, Co. Tipperary. Church of Ireland church. North side of tomb–chest under Archer (?) effigies. c.1520 (?)
Catalogue number 246b

327 Thurles, Co. Tipperary. Church of Ireland church. South side of tomb–chest under Archer (?) effigies. c.1520 (?)
Catalogue number 246c

328 Thurles, Co. Tipperary. Church of Ireland church. Head end–slab of tomb–chest under Archer (?) effigies. c.1520 (?)
Catalogue number 246d

329 Thurles, Co. Tipperary. Church of Ireland church. East end-slab of tomb-chest of Archer (?) tomb. c.1520 (?)
Catalogue number 246e

330 Holycross Abbey, Co. Tipperary. End-slab from a tomb-chest. Mid-16th century.
Catalogue number 240

331 Inistioge, Co. Kilkenny. Catholic church. Fragment of a tomb-chest. 16th century.
Catalogue number 111

332 Mothel, Co. Waterford. Tomb-chest. The south side. c.1500.
Catalogue number 251a

333 Mothel, Co. Waterford. Tomb-chest. The east end. c.1500.
Catalogue number 251b

334 Mothel, Co. Waterford. Tomb-chest. The west end. c. 1500.
Catalogue number 251c

335 Mothel, Co. Waterford. Tomb-chest. The north side. c. 1500.
Catalogue number 251d

336 Clonmel, Co. Tipperary. Fragment of a tomb-front in wall near west end of church. First half 16th century.
Catalogue number 238

337 Lismore Cathedral, Co. Waterford. The MacCragh
tomb. East end and south side. 1557.
Catalogue number 250b & d

338 Lismore Cathedral, Co. Waterford. The MacCragh tomb. The west end. 1557.
Catalogue number 250c

340 Kilcormac, Co. Offaly.
Crucifixion. Late 16th century.
Catalogue number 210

339 Johnstown, Co. Kilkenny. Crucifixion. 16th century.
Catalogue number 126

Topographical Index of Plates

(References are to plate numbers)